Linstrom

PRAYERS FROM THE BURNED-OUT CITY

PRAYERS
from the Burned-Out City

ROBERT W. CASTLE, JR.

SHEED AND WARD: NEW YORK

To a group of young men once known as "The Nations,"
who are now the hope of a new nation.

CONTENTS

Prayers over the City . . .

A LITANY

O God, the City for people to live and work in and to know one
another,

     Help us to love the City.

O God, the Metropolis of all men's lives,

     Help us to love the Metropolis.

O God, who lives in tenements, who goes to segregated schools,
who is beaten in precincts, who is unemployed,

     Help us to know you.

O God, who hangs on street corners, who tastes the grace of
cheap wine and the sting of the needle,

     Help us to know you.

O God, who can't write or read, who is on welfare, and who is
treated like garbage,

     Help us to know you.

O God, who lives and no one knows his name and who knows
that he is nobody,

     Help us to know you.

O God, whose name is spik, nigger, ginny, and kike,

     Help us to know you.

13

O God, who pays too much rent for a lousy apartment because
he speaks Spanish,

> Help us to know you.

O God, who is uprooted by Urban Renewal and removed from
your neighborhood,

> Help us to know you.

O God, who is cold in the slums of winter,

> Help us to touch you.

O God, who is children in the grave burned in the tenement fire,

> Help us to hear your cry.

O God, whose church down the street closed and moved away,

> Help us to touch you.

O God, who is tired of his church and its ministers and priests,
irrelevant and unbloody,

> Help us to join you.

O God, whose elected leaders only know you exist at election
time and represent themselves and not the people,

> Help us to touch you.

O God, whose local papers distort the truth, never listen to you,
but represent the comfortable and powerful,

> Help us to hear you.

O God, who is poor and has all sorts of programs being planned
for you, and people to speak for you out of both sides of their
mouth,

> Help us to be with you.

O God, who is sold a bill of goods by phony white liberals,

> Help us to stand with you.

O God, whose enemy is white, powerful and deaf, dumb and
blind,

> Help us to stand with you.

O God, who is spoken for by black established leaders whom the
people do not know,

Help us to stand with you.
O God, who has leaders, black and white, who sell you out,
Help us to be with you.
O God, who couldn't take it any longer and was in the streets last summer, and was called a hoodlum, communist, agitator, bum, wino, drug addict,
Help us to know you.
O God, who carries a sign, sits on the ground, strikes his rent, boycotts the store,
Help us to join you.
O God, who is fed up with it all and who is determined to do something, who is organizing people for power to change the world.
Help us to join you.
O God, who has had it and dreams of a new day and is on the march across the land that he might make his own destiny,
Help us to join you.

A PLACE TO SLEEP

Jesus, you understand.
There were many nights
   when you didn't have any special place to sleep.
Your mother and father told you
   about the day you were born,
   and they didn't have a place to rest or sleep.
Well, Lord, here in the city
   there are a lot of men and women
   created in your image
   who have no place to sleep tonight.
They aren't looking for anything special.
Maybe just a flop
   or an abandoned car someplace
   where it's a little warm in winter and somewhat safe.
A place to dream of better days gone by
   perhaps forever
   or a brighter day tomorrow.
So, Lord, watch over everyone tonight
   who doesn't know where to sleep.

May they have rest
    and may their rest be good for the next day.
And one day we will all sleep in you.
Good night, Jesus.
Amen.

TENEMENT FIRES

Did you hear those sirens last night, Lord?
They sound like lamentations.
You can hear the cry come unto you.
"Save the children . . . Save the children . . ."
Seven of the children died in the fire on Whiton Street.
All huddled up against the windows.
Dead.
A lot of people die
        in the fires of slums and tenements in the city.
A lot of people lose
        what little furniture and clothing they own.
When you live in the firetraps of the city,
        there is never any insurance.

Lord, the fire kept burning up the stairs . . .
        up the stairs, Lord!
There wasn't any fire escape
        and the stairs, Lord, just weren't there any more.
They were so scared, Lord,

so scared they couldn't move any more—
     seven children and their mother.
All that smoke—
     they couldn't breathe.
The landlord and the city inspector
     had choked off the air long ago.
Lord, you know that's no way to have to live and die—with no
air to breathe.
Going to bed at night
     not knowing if you will be alive in the morning.
All that crummy wiring and those kerosene stoves.
Once it starts, that's it, Lord.
So, Lord, this prayer
     is about helping the people to organize in these firetraps,
     not to pay any rent
     until the owner and the city get with it.
Help us to sleep safe tonight—
     the sirens still,
     the children in your ever-loving arms.
Suffer the little children, Lord.
Amen.

PEOPLE ARE SCARED

A whole lot of people are scared, Lord,
    just plain scared.
You know why?
The "Man" has got a lot of people thinking scared—
    brainwashed into thinking they can't do anything to change
things
    like changing schools, jobs, houses,
    the cops, City Hall,
    and just lots of things.
Making people think they are nobody and powerless
    is the work of the devil, Lord.
That's what we call the "Man" lots of times, Lord—
    the devil.
I'm praying real hard and loud that we are all somebody.
You're in us, ain't you, Lord?
I can just feel you in me.
Lots of times I get in your way
    but I feel you.
And I feel you getting to me and saying:

20

No more being scared.
The Lord ain't scared—never has been—never will be.
No more scared.
I got the power, Lord—
    I got you and I'm somebody.
Oh Lord,
I'm somebody so damned special and important that I'm on my
way.
I'm on my way up to the "devil man," Lord,
    and I'm going to wrestle him down like you did.
Remember?
You remember!
And I'm going to win the "Man"
    like you won the devil.
The angels are going to come and minister to me.
Bless those angels, Lord.
Amen.

RENT STRIKES

Alleluia, Lord!
Alleluia, Lord! Alleluia!
Hear our joy.
We thank you for making us men and making us women
    and making us people.
Alleluia, Lord!
We feel the joy and know we are one tonight, Lord.
One flesh—one image—
    the image of you, Lord.
It's been so long since I felt this joy, Lord,
    I just have to tell you about it.
We were all like fingers without a hand—
    you know, just a finger here and there, joined to nothing.
A finger without a hand ain't able to do much.
There just wasn't anything we could do.
Then it happened, Lord. Alleluia!
That S.O.B. of a landlord—
    you know, Lucifer's friend—
    didn't pay his gas and light bill and they cut the heat

and we all froze real cold for three days in the dump
we live in,
> paying $95.00 a month.
And, Lord, then little by little
> the fingers started coming together,
> and pretty soon we organized.
We started meeting and talking about how something had to be
done.
Like we weren't going to let the Man walk over us no more.
No more, Lord.
And we became a hand.
And then tonight, Lord, it happened—it happened right there
sitting and talking and praying and planning.
That hand made a fist.
Those fingers just came together and made a fist
> and we stuck that fist right in the Man's face and said,
> "No rent, Man,
> No rent, Man, until everything is right."
It was the fist of justice.
It was the fist of love.
Alleluia, Lord! Alleluia!
Amen.

IT'S SUMMER, LORD

It's summer, Lord.
You know—like hot, smelly, dirty soft tar,
    noise and no air to breathe.
Seems like us and the kids never got no air to breathe.
In the winter that damn kerosene stove takes all the air
    and in the summer,
        well, there ain't that much air for all of us.
We all got lots of things to do in the summer, Lord.
Wet sit outside the house
    and watch the trucks and buses
    and our kids dodge 'em.
We listen to the noise
    and surrender to the sweat and stink and dirt.
Maybe the cops will come down and mess up a good party or two
    and then the music and laughter of the street will stop
    and screams and cussing will replace the dullness of it all.
But it's the kids, Lord.
That's what I really wanted to talk to you about—the kids.
And the program, Lord—the goddamn program.

24

I can't do nothin' for my kids—
    it seems like I can never do nothin' for my kids.
Some case workers, some preachers, some city recreation kid
who hustled his job through the old man and the old system
    always got to be doing something for my kids.
Now don't get me wrong, Lord. I ain't against my kids doing
something—I just would like to be able to do it for them and
with them.
My kids don't need the program, Lord—
    they need me.
O Christ,
    I want to be able to do something for my kids—
    take them away for a little while,
    change this lousy summer into trees and grass and clean
water and fish and music and laughing and no cops.
Give me air, Lord . . .
Give me room, Lord . . .
Give me a chance, Lord . . .
Give me my daily bread, Lord
    and I'll take care of the summer.
Amen.

DAILY BREAD

All these years I've been praying,
"Give us this day our daily bread . . ."
I used to think that meant like bread—
    food you know, Lord.
But here in these United States
    it means money, Lord—
    real money.
We call it dough—
    that's money
    and that's what you make bread with.
Bread is money, Lord,
    and I ain't got my daily bread in so long I can't do a damn
thing for myself.

So Lord,
I'm counting on you
    and I'm organizing myself for some dust—some iron—
some bread, Lord.
Just my daily bread—

26

and then I'll take care of business the way you intended me
to do.
Deliver us from this evil, Lord,
    and we will all have bread—
    beautiful bread like you meant, Lord.
Amen.

NATIVITY

I had a baby last night, Lord.
I know you know because he is your child.
You know what I mean, Lord:
    we are all your babies.
Like Joseph and Mary laid down and loved one another and
made your baby Jesus,
    that is how Juan and I made our baby.
He is a sweet child, Lord.
A big baby, Lord,
    and I am only fifteen.
He hurt me but I hardly remember now; he is so beautiful.
How old was Mary
    when she had her first child, Lord?
Maybe about my age.
Joseph married her when she was going to have the baby.
My mother would not let me marry Juan.
She says I am too young.
Things are much different now you know, Lord.
Some people think my baby is dirty and I am dirty because I
have no husband.

I do not think I am dirty.
I have only love for my baby and his father—
     and for you, Lord, who make all the babies.
Lord, do you think everyone would have thought that Jesus was
dirty and his mother Mary if Joseph did not marry her?
I would not think they were dirty.
I would have still loved them very much,
     like they have loved me.
Thank you, Lord, for the baby.
I love you so much tonight.
Amen.

THE DESERT

Lord, I figure you were lonely out there in that wilderness thing.
Being alone—
    I mean like with no one to touch
    or to touch you.
There just weren't any people.
Here in the city there are lots of people
    but some people might just as well be in some wilderness.
People live in one lousy room on maybe $57 a month,
    and that's like fasting forty days and forty nights.
When they can get out they might just stand around Journal
Square,
    looking into faces no one sees,
    or grab a cheap taste
    and then back to that room, those walls,
    that one window that everybody goes by going somewhere
to someone.
Nobody really gives a damn about you.
You're just there until they find you one morning, dead.
Do the angels come then and minister to you?

Lord, I don't know.
I hope so.
Damn it, I hope so.
Amen.

A LITTLE PRAYER

This is just a little prayer, Lord, for all the little people who run this city.
Little in their hearts,
    little in their minds,
    little in their love—
    real little people.
How little can they get, Lord?
Give us a little luck, Lord.
Help us to get them out of the big offices.
Amen.

THE ADDICT

If you're a drug addict, Lord,
      they've got a lot of things in the city to help you.
First they make you carry a card saying you're an addict or were
an addict.
It means the same thing to the cops and most of the people here.
And then they got this huge city hospital with two-thirds of its
beds closed down because the crooks stole so much money for so
long that now there is no bed for you if you need help.
Some preacher told me to go to the Medical Center when I
wanted some help.
Like a goddamned fool I went.
The cops arrested me—because I wanted help, I guess.
I did 30 days.
Lord, this preacher told me you're alive.
They all say that about you—you're alive.
I know that, Lord,
      and I want to say to you, Lord, I love you.
So don't come by here,
      they'll give you 30 days.
Amen.

FOR CROOKS

This prayer is for all the crooks in the city.
It should be a big prayer, Lord,
    because there are a whole lot of crooks.
First of all, Lord,
    there are all the little crooks who are getting caught every
day:
    the poor who cheat or break, snatch a pocketbook—
    you know.
Then, Lord, there are a lot more big crooks
    who steal more in a week than the little crooks steal in a
lifetime.
You know:
    some politicians, businessmen, judges, policemen, loan
sharks, all the big-time bookies and numbers racketeers . . .
The Mayor, if he wants to play his number,
    can put his money down right in City Hall.
Then the money don't have to travel too far.
I heard, Lord, that they even got mental patients at the County
hospital collecting slips.

34

It might be good therapy, but I don't dig the guys who are getting
rich.
Now, Lord, these are the good people of our city
     who tell the people that they are going to uphold law and
order.
All that money they get, Lord, helps push corruption in
government, industry, schools, dope, you name it.
They're usually pretty responsible people with nice homes,
     good clothes and fine cars.
They eat in the right restaurants and go to the best shows.
You know what else, Lord?
They usually go to church every Sunday, speak at Communion
breakfasts and are known as your followers.
Now you know they're not your followers;
     but the church never says anything about what they do
     so most people think they must be okay with you and your
church.
Sad, ain't it, Lord?
Real sad.
I don't think the crooks are going to last too long, Lord.
Everything is crumbling all around them—
     the whole system is cracking up all over the country.
You can sense it.
They're getting scared.
They keep buying more weapons and becoming more oppressive.
The good guys—
     that's what they think they are.
But they're scared, Lord.
It would be good if they could change.
I wish they could.
They need to be free too.
Amen.

35

POLICE BRUTALITY

Lord, the world has been violent a long time.
We all know that.
But that doesn't mean we should be content with violence.
A lot of people—you know, black people,
 Spanish-speaking people, poor people—are always getting
their heads beat in by the cops.
Now, Lord, I guess we have to have police,
 but move their hearts to stop beating people in jail houses,
precinct back alleys, waterfronts and dark country roads.
There just isn't any sense to police brutality, Lord.
The keepers of the law ought to obey the law, too.
Help them to be good examples.
You know some of them are always on the take and payoffs.
Help them to stop helping organized crime and catch some of
 the real crooks for a change.
We are all praying that one day—one day real soon—all men will
be treated fairly and their rights will be respected by the police.
Now that's only fair, isn't it, Lord?
No more beatings, no more forced confessions, no more payoffs

36

    by the big-time crooks.
Let the law be the law in honesty and truth.
That would be good, wouldn't it?
Justice.
Amen.

THE JUDGES

Remember, Lord, when you raised up those judges
    to set things right?
That was a long time ago now, Lord,
    when the judges set the people free from their strife and
bondage.
We've got some judges now, Lord,
    who were raised up by crooked politicians to keep your
people in prison.
City Hall tells them who to put away and who to set free.
If you've got money, Lord, you can go free anytime you want,
    and if you've got enough money and know the right people
you can get out of trouble in a hurry.
Poor people, oppressed people,
    know why there are judges now, Lord—
    to keep them poor and oppressed.
With whatever you judge, some day you're going to be judged.
They say you said that, Lord.
That day can't come too soon, Lord.
When it comes I hope you and the people will raise up the judges,

and for Christ's sake, no more of the same, but some good judges.
Amen.

THEY SAID
THEY WOULD KILL ME

Lord, a lot of people have called on the phone over the years to
say they would kill me.
Some have said they were going to get my kids, too.
And just the other day a fellow-priest
     told me a group of policemen said they would kill me this
summer if there was any trouble in the city.

I heard Billy Graham the other night.
He said the cops were sent by God.
I know I'm going to die someday, Lord.
And I don't mind being with you at all Lord,
     because that is why I am living anyway.
What I'm trying to say is,
     I don't need all that protection, at least not right now.
If you are sending those cops, Lord, you don't have to send any
more.
There are enough of them to kill a whole lot of us now.
Spare us from the cops, Lord.

And you take us one day, your day,
        to your ever-loving arms, Lord.
Amen.

THE BIG CLEANUP

Lord, why don't we white people cut it out?
I mean,
    like running down to some poor neighborhood with our brooms and mops and paint and soap to clean up some street.
Why don't we clean up our own mess?
Can't we see our own dirt or smell our own stink?
If we are going to do anything,
    why don't we get out of the way of the people who are doing something for themselves?
You talked about that, Lord, some time ago—
    about taking big pieces of wood out of our own eye before looking around for splinters in other people's eyes.
Spare the people from us, Lord.
And help us to clean up our own things.
You would like that Lord.
Amen.

THE GRAPES OF WRATH

Lord, when you went up to that Golden City of Jerusalem
    and saw all that money, and the priests hawk that stuff
outside the Temple getting rich
    and remembered all those hungry people—
    you went into that violent thing and turned over tables and
put it on them.

Lord, when I see what I get
    and my brothers and sisters get
    and two blocks away there is all that money and people with
fine things and vacations and nice houses and fat jobs—
    I go into that violent thing too.
They crucified you.
What do you think they're going to do to me, Lord?
You got to believe it.
Amen.

O GOD, THE CITY

O God, who still is,
    Help us to be.
O God, who is full of guts to be,
    Help us to join you.
O God, who is all men joined together in all peace, all truth,
all justice, all love,
    Help us to love you.
O God, the City,
    We need you.
O God, the City,
    We need you.
O God, the Holy City,
    We love you.

Pro Pauperibus . . .

A LITANY

O God, who is old, and lives on fifty dollars a month, in one crummy room and can't get outside,

    Help us to see you.

O God, who is white and lives with Mr. Charlie, who is black and lives with Uncle Tom,

    Help us to see you.

O God, who lives in the projects created by Federal, State and City indifference,

    Help us to see you.

O God, who is fifteen in the sixth grade,

    Help us to touch you.

O God, who is three and whose belly aches in hunger,

    Help us to touch you.

O God, whose toys are broken bottles, tin cans, whose playyard is garbage and debris, and whose playhouse is the floors of the condemned buildings,

    Help us to touch you.

O God, who sleeps in a bed with his four brothers and sisters, and who cries and no one hears him,

Help us to touch you.

O God, who has no place to sleep tonight except an abandoned car, an alley or deserted building,

Help us to touch you.

O God, who is uneducated, unskilled, unwanted, and unemployed,

Help us to know you.

O God, who was laid off last week and can't pay the rent or feed the kids,

Help us to be with you.

O God, who is a bum, a chisler, who is lazy, because people say you are when you don't work and you want to work and you can't find a job,

Help us to be with you.

O God, who always gets the sweatshop jobs for a lousy buck and a quarter,

Help us to know you.

O God, all poor at Welfare being told you don't want to work,

Help us to be with you.

O God, whose job at the factory is gone because the factory closed and left the city,

Help us to know you.

O God, whose union has a sweetheart contract with the employer and you get double-dealed every day.

Help us to know you.

O God, who smells and has no place to bathe,

Help us to be with you.

O God, who is dressed by the suburbs from the church clothing store,

Help us to touch you.

O God, who is chased by the cops, who sits in jail for seven months with no charges brought, waiting for the Grand Jury and no money for bail,

> Help us to know you.

O God, whose blood is red, whose skin is black, whose red blood is on the billy club,

> Help us to touch you.

O God, who hustles fifty cents for lousy wine, who sells copper and lead to clean his clothes,

> Help us to touch you.

O God, who pushes a baby carriage at night to the cans of another's garbage and claims it as his treasure,

> Help us to know you.

O God, who works all day, who feeds and cares for her children at night and dreams of better days, and is alone,

> Help us to know you.

O God, who works all day for bare survival and is still poor and humiliated by landlord, employer and government,

> Help us to know you.

O God, who is without power, voiceless, who has no share in his destiny,

> Help us to join you.

O God, who is unorganized, and without strength to change his world, his metropolis, his city, his neighborhood,

> Help us to join you.

DOES IT HAVE TO BE
THAT WAY, LORD?

Does it always have to be that way, Lord?
They tell me it always has to be that way.
I don't really believe it,
      but I can't find anything or anyone but you to prove that it
doesn't have to be that way.
You know—
      the wheelers and dealers, the schemers, the sellouts and
buy-ins;
      you know, like it can't be honest and right; it has to be sick.
I don't know any more, Lord.
There are so many people saying they got something going for
me, but all I see is that they got something going for them.
Like there's a new program now—
      they call it Anti-Poverty, Lord,
      because I think they're against my being poor.
I've always been against my being poor, Lord.
Now they got a lot of people making big money to get me out
of being poor.

They tell we where I can get jobs for $1.25 an hour and where
to get surplus food and get on welfare and legal advice and how
my kids can get a head start—for what I don't know—and where
to get training for jobs where there ain't no jobs and all those
kind of things.

Well, I appreciate that, Lord, I really do.

Just the same I get hungry,

and I get cold,

and I get broke.

And I have the feeling they're wheeling and dealing with me and
nothing's really changing around here.

The people who made us poor and have kept us poor are pretty
much the same people who are running the program.

I kind of have the feeling, Lord,

they need me in this program more than I need to be in it.

Is it always going to be that way, Lord?

I just don't know any more.

I need something, Lord,

I need something real bad.

So bad, I could cry;

so bad I could scream;

so bad I could die for it.

As a matter of fact,

I will die for it, Lord,

I will!

Amen.

THREE DAYS, LORD

Three days, Lord,
    that's all I lasted.
I wanted to quit that first night,
    but I lasted three days.
It was at the chemical factory—where you wear the masks
because it ain't fit breathing there, Lord.
I worked that midnight shift to 8:00 a.m.
Twenty minutes for lunch and no breaks.
Just working on the grit soap and the insecticide and the ammonia and the acid.
There was no singing,
    just working hard, Lord, for $1.25 an hour.
Three days, Lord.
Did you hear, Lord, what they're doing?
They're taking a buck-fifty a night for the union—
    seven-fifty a week, Lord.
Nobody ever knows who the union is.
The bosses don't care.
The union don't care.

That puts the working man in some spot, Lord.
You got to be in it to believe it.
It was Thanksgiving Day, Lord,
    8:00 in the morning,
    and the man called our names and said come to the office.
We were laid off, Lord.
You kind of give thanks not to have to work there any more.
But you need a job.
You need even that bit of money.
It's something to do.
Christmas is coming soon.
I lasted three days.
Maybe they will call next week, they said.
I hope they don't call before I get a better job.
Lord, I'm praying I get a better job before they call.
I want to work.
Amen.

I just came back from the Unemployment, Lord.

PEOPLE SLEEPING AGAIN, LORD

People sleeping again, Lord.
We have been sleeping so long.
Well, we were all sleeping again.
This time it was on the floor of the Anti-Poverty Program office.
The floor up there is hard, Lord—real hard.
Almost as hard as the people who have been running the program.
The people who run the program are big-timers—phony, Lord—
    politicians, lawyers, businessmen, preachers and all those types.
The poor people ain't running nothing.
That's why we took over that poverty office.
We have been here over a day and we ain't seen too many of the big boys up here.
We ain't sleeping no more, Lord,
    except maybe on some floors up here and at Welfare and the Board of Education and City Hall.
They all got hard floors and hard heads and hearts too, Lord.

My prayer is to ask you to keep us all awake now.
Remember, Lord, when your mother had to come in and say,
"Wake up, little Jesus, it's time to get up and work with your father."
Help us to work with the father of us all.
All working together to change this city—
poor people like you were poor, Lord,
together loving the brothers and sisters and making no peace
until your kingdom comes on earth as it is in heaven for ever and ever.
Amen.

HUNGRY

Dear Jesus,
     you remember that long time you were in the wilderness?
You had nothing to eat or drink.
You must have been real hungry—
     so hungry you were tempted to turn stone into bread.
There are a lot of people hungry in the city, Lord.
Little children.
Real poor people.
Real hungry.
Lord, we ain't praying for you to make the stones into bread.
We are praying that the hungry may have a chance to make their
own bread.

You must still be hungry, Lord,
     because so many of your children are hungry.
Your belly must be huge in emptiness;
     your eyes bulging;
     you're real hungry, Lord . . .
I was hungry and you gave me to eat . . .
Amen.

A HIT

I made a big hit today, Lord—
    and the son of a bitch took off on me.

My mother moved into a different rat trap on Ocean Ave—
    that's an ocean of dirt, hustlers and pimps, swanky funeral
houses for the dead and dumps for the living.
Well, she moved into 376 Ocean.
I thought maybe I should play that number and play a buck.
It's the only way you can make a big hit if you're poor.
Now I make a big hit and the numbers man takes off on me—
    son of a bitch!
That ain't right, Lord.
Amen.

POOR RICHARD'S ALMANAC

Lord,
    I am tired of hearing about how the rich worked hard to get rich
    and how hard the affluent work to stay affluent.
Now that's a damned lie, Lord.
If hard work—real labor—
    getting up early, and coming home exhausted at night,
    is some kind of great virtue and makes you affluent,
    then, Lord, I've got to tell you the poor would all be rich, right now.
Only the poor work hard, Lord—
    in lousy junkyards, sweatshops, laundries, emptying bed pans—
    I see the poor walking and getting on buses to go to work at 6:00 a. m.
Not the affluent.
It's the poor who come home tired and dirty.
The poor don't have two or three hour lunches, or vacations,
    or bonuses, or benefits, or decent and safe surroundings to work in.

58

And when you're poor, Lord,
     somebody is watching to see if you're working all the time.
Are you watching too, Lord?
I hope you are.
Amen.

Amen.

LAST NIGHT

Lord, I went to sleep last night with a man.
I hadn't slept with a man in so long.
He said he loves me.
But I don't know.
I have three babies now, Lord.
I hope we didn't make a baby because I am not supposed to have
any sex.
I'm on welfare.
Amen.

I'M STRUGGLING, LORD

I'm struggling, Lord—struggling—struggling.
There are so many things to struggle for,
    so many Jerusalem roads to walk.
So many battles to wage, people to fight.
So many who just don't care,
    don't have any real feeling for their brothers—
    no love, Lord.
It makes you mad.
You hear them say like, "Wait! Wait for the Lord."
Wait for you? Crazy!
You already came and are here now.
What's there to wait for, Lord?
Waiting for truth and justice and love is like never.
They say I'm impatient—unrealistic—don't know how to be
satisfied.
I ain't satisfied at all, Lord—
    I'm just hungry.
My heart and head are so hungry for us all to love one another
and to get with it.

I'm sorry, Lord, for being so damned mad at so many people and
fighting so many things all the time, but I can't see any other way.
Until the kingdom comes—

    your kingdom, Lord, and mine and everybody's.

The kingdom of love.

Thank you Lord, for your struggle, your road up to Jerusalem.

I couldn't walk mine if I didn't know you already walked the
road before me,

    took up the cross and won.

Is there any other way, Lord?

O Lord, is there any other way?

I love you, I love the brothers and sisters,

    I love the enemy—

    at least I want to love them.

Help me to fight on and love them too.

Their souls stink real bad, Lord—but you love them.

Amen.

LOVE THE SICK

A lot of poor people who are sick, Lord,
      don't have private doctors to call up to come around to see
them, or nice comfortable offices to go to get well.
When they are sick or their baby is sick,
      they have to go to the emergency rooms or the clinics of the
city hospitals.
We are grateful for all the clinics and things, Lord,
      but you know sometimes people have to wait for hours and
hours while they're sick and in pain.
Lots of times when you're real sick, they don't put you in the
hospital.
Lots of babies get sent home still sick
      and sometimes they die because their care was so little.
Now, Lord, this doesn't happen to rich people or important
people.
It happens to poor people.
Now you were very poor and so were your friends,
      so you know what it's all about.
The poor aren't asking for any favors, just what's right:

some real care and real interest—
and even a little love wouldn't hurt.
You helped the sick who came to you in faith.
Amen.

A MAN WAS CRYING

A man was crying today, Lord.
It's hard to see a man cry.
But sometimes you feel something so deeply you just have to cry.
You cried over Jerusalem.
Well, this man was crying over another city.
A city which said,
    "If you don't work, man, you're nobody, you're nothing."
That ain't right, Lord.
If we're made in your image, how can we be nobody?
I don't like to hear people saying you're nobody, Lord.
Help us all to work, Lord,
    to work and to be paid fair,
    and if we don't work, Lord,
    in a world where there are just fewer and fewer jobs,
    help everybody to know that each of us has the same value.
Now I don't just mean the same value in your eyes;
    I mean in everybody's eyes.
That's love,
    and that's what you are, Lord.

So that's the way it's got to be.
We are all somebody—we are all you, Lord.
Let our tears this night be sweet in that joy.
Thank you, Lord, that's real good news.
Amen.

BAIL MONEY

I got a letter the other day from this guy.
He is sitting in the county jail.
He's been in the county jail for four months now; he was a
witness to a fight that a guy got hurt real bad in
    and so he is a material witness, they say.
So they put him in jail and put $500 bail on him.
Now he's poor and only eighteen and no parents living
    and the only thing he knows is he hasn't got no material—
    like $55 to buy bail
    so he is just sitting for four months,
    for nothing,
    because he has nothing.
Somebody stole a million bucks in some kind of soy bean oil.
He had a big $20,000 bail, but he walked out of the jail.
You sit in jail, Lord, for four months because you haven't got
$55 and then see how you feel.
Justice in this city, Lord, is a bad justice.
I hope this whole thing gets changed around.
It will when a whole lot of people who keep poor people in jail
get put in jail.

I hope there will be justice
and that they've got some bail money.
Amen.

PEOPLE BUYING GUNS

People buying guns, Lord.
Bang, bang, you're dead!
Like hurry up and bleed and die.
White people got lots of guns—
        got the police—got the army,
        and they're getting ready
        in case any of those niggers heard of Nat Turner or George
Washington
        and decide to fight the oppressor.

If a man is getting killed and oppressed
        what should he do, Lord? Should he kind of just take it and
suffer peacefully?
A lot of people have done that for a long time.
You suffered peacefully after they caught you, and you were
beautiful.
I hope I can be that beautiful after they catch me Lord, if they
ever do.
Should I suffer peacefully,

or fight back, defend myself,
     like take up arms like our fathers did a long time ago and
then told the people they have a right to revolution if they are
oppressed.
Should I take up my gun and follow the revolution,
     or take up my cross and follow you?
I know it's all the same, Lord.
Either way I'm going to die for justice and human dignity.
All I ask now is for you to help me to live and die
For something worthwhile—
     like you did.
Amen.

THE SHORT STORY

You know man this is my story. It's about the night I died and how they laid me here in the ground. It isn't a long story, but it's my story. I'm cold bones in the ground now man, but it's my story. The story lasted for sixteen years, but it all got squeezed into a couple of days in the end. I died early. But nobody told me I was dead. So you know, for sixteen years I made it. I had lots of brothers and sisters and a father and a mother. My father, he died too. My mother, I loved her. She drank a lot; like she drank and talked about how we were somebody. We were always somebody when my mother drank too much. And I went to school. I made a table in shop once; the man he helped and it was good. I made it man. And it was good.

I went to church too. I was baptized—and the sisters used to teach us about Jesus. Sweet Jesus, Bloody Jesus, Good Jesus, My Jesus. I went to church. And I got into trouble man. I was in the gang. I was in the Youth House cause you know the man picked me up. I drank wine man and got sick and puked all over. All those years alive, sometimes happy, sometimes high, sometimes good, sometimes bad, and, you know man, I was dead and nobody, nobody, told me.

Well shoot, I'm just one of many guys who were alive and didn't know they were dead. It all happened that night. Remember it was getting warm. May, you know; trees, flowers, grass, people on the street, the air even comes through all the soot and stink. It's warm, and school will end soon, and then there'll be nothing to do. Like you stand around and nothing man, nothing. The church was still having all those dances on Saturdays. It was something to do—to feel a girl, to sneak in a little wine—have some fun, maybe there would be a turnout. We wanted it cool though, cause they were our dances. I made the dance early. Some of the guys were there but not too many, they would come later. I came to the dance alone cause I had some other ideas. There was a setup, on the hill, I would make later.

I had come up to the church like I always did. Out of the project. There was nothing doing there. The rec hall was a wreck man, and it never was open. So I went out of the project, where only us black people lived, and walked along Grand Street. I don't know the cat who called it Grand Street. But man, he must have been sick. Along Grand Street the girls were out early, some of the guys were hustling wine, a taste of heaven at the end of the day, shared in the halls of piss in one of the condemned buildings. The lights were as dull as ever. Lots of people were getting food for tomorrow, from the dingy stores of white people and high prices, like we weren't poor enough. On the corner I ran it off the mouth with a couple of guys. They would get a couple of more tastes before making it to the dance. Then it was the walk up the hill, like walking up to heaven, if there is a heaven. It's not so far but, damn the hill, it's steep.

So I'm at the dance and I gotta make it now, further up the hill, near the cut, you know, where the trains used to go and now there is only garbage. It was at the cut, man, where I got it.

I went too far up on the hill. I was off my turf. You know, like you belong down the hill and they belong on the hill. Crazy you know—just crazy. But that was the way it was and I knew it, and I tried to make this set but they wouldn't let me in. One word led to another, you know how it goes, and then I was running.

Running, I was running man since I was a baby. We were all running. We learned to run from the Man. To run from job to job, from tenement to tenement, from rats to rats, four-legged and two-legged. We ran from the enemy; white, soft, comfortable, big, powerful; from them we ran. It would pain too much not to run. So we ran; we ran from self, from whom we were and where we came from.

I was running again and I was scared. They caught me at the cut. I fell. I was scared. Then I got it. It was cold, like living on Grand Street in the winter, when the snow comes in the windows and in the halls, and the kerosene stinks heat, and you're cold in the bones. The blade shot through my chest, went to my heart and through it, till it came out the other side. It didn't hurt. It was just cold, like it had always been cold. I felt no pain. No more, no less, than all the pain those years. You see, it couldn't hurt me anymore; the school, no jobs, the cops, the landlords, the crooks at City Hall, the garbage, the church, all the good people in the city, had killed me long ago and I didn't know it. Now all the death of sixteen years went through my head and started to come out of my heart.

I didn't have to run anymore. They were running. Running like hell, away from me. I could hear them running. And I was alone. It was quiet, laying there in the cut. Then I heard the sirens. They were coming for me. It would be the last time they came for me. They were here and, like when I was a baby, somebody picked me up and made me warm.

Everybody was talking like crazy and running all around me and the lights burned down on me. They were trying to save my life. There were doctors and nurses and they were trying to save my life. How can you save a life—a body and a soul—that is already dead? Why did they want to save me now? Why not when I was five, or ten, or last week? "Why now?", I wanted to shout. "I'm dead—let me go."

You know, I wanted to laugh; they didn't know my name. How do you like that? They didn't know my name or where I lived. They didn't know my mother or brothers, or my sisters, or my church. They didn't know my name and now, when it was like sixteen years too late, they wanted to save me, without a name.

The lights and voices were getting further and further away. I wasn't scared. I didn't feel anything. Man, then I heard it. I heard my name. Somebody knew my name and my address and my mother and my brothers and sisters. It was the Father from the church. He knew my name. My mother and brothers would come now. I could see the Father only dimly. But I could see the Father. He was talking to me and I could hear him; he was like praying—he touched me and, I don't know how, but I spoke. Man, you know what I said? I said, "Father, don't worry, I ain't gonna die." I said that man. I was dead and I said that. Now my mother and brothers were there, but they took me away, to where the lights were brighter. I went to sleep now, peacefully, quietly, and I would speak no more.

It was hours later, in a crummy room, on what floor I don't know, that somebody said, "He is dead." You know, like some great discovery. Like they just found out that, on a hot May morning, about 4:00 a.m., I was dead.

Then they all went through the bit of crying, and the Father, he was praying, and my mother held me like she used to, and my brothers swore and rushed out into the night. I was D.E.A.D. It wasn't my secret anymore. Now everybody knew.

For a couple of days things got all mixed up. All the guys wanted to burn somebody up on the hill. It's all crazy, you know. They finally killed a kid, fifteen, just walking on the street— they didn't know who he was. They cut him and he died, and his mother cried, and all that. It was always screwed up like that; next month they would forget and be friends again and laugh, man, until all that frustration built up, and you had to hit somebody again. Even the city, the big guys, everybody, got kinda shook up, and they had meetings, like maybe something should be done to change things. But they just talked. And then they even stopped talking. Some kook on the hill tried to burn the Father and some guys, with a hand grenade—but he didn't throw it. Things got real bad, and the cops were everywhere.

You know the cops came that day, when they closed the lid on the box and planted me in the ground. They were lined up the hill, from Grand Street to Summit Avenue and the church. The church is on Summit. Like you have made it. And the cops, on horses and in cars, were all along Summit. And the cats, man, that made the funeral. Hundreds and hundreds came. A lot of the guys were searched when they came in. The cops, they were in church. I never knew cops went to church. Everybody from school came. It was late in the morning when they carried me for that last ride. I was going from Sullivan's Funeral Home. That was the old tough talk on the street—"You wanna go to Sullivan's?"—I had said it a hundred times, to a hundred guys. Now I was in Sullivan's.

We made the trip down from Sullivan's kinda slow. There were lots of cars behind. My mother and brothers and sisters rode right behind me. I rode and they rode in shiny, big, black Cadillacs. We were always poor. I was poor, man. Hungry lots of times. Nothing in your pocket, to get your clothes clean, or catch a show, or even a lousy taste. We were poor. Now we rode in big, black, swanky, cars for one long ride to church and grave, and then back to the roaches and the rats and the hopelessness of it all.

Slow, slow, all the way to the church. Then, the line of cops—silently standing there wishing that all the black bastards—that's what they call us—were in the box with me. Damn it. And then, all the guys hustling into the church, and the Father standing up at the top of the stairs. I couldn't figure the Father. I liked him. At least I think I liked him. I had to con him—we all had to con him, you know. He was a white, man, what do you expect? Now I don't know if he is in the box with me, with his sweet, smelly, Jesus or whether, like some of the other Fathers, he'll get out of the box. You know, he can get out of the box when he wants to. I don't know yet. I wanted to ask the Father why he didn't tell me I was dead when I was happy playing in the gym or dancing or singing a hymn. Why didn't you tell me Father, I wondered.

Well, I told the Father that night I would be in church soon. Man, I didn't think it would be this soon. Up the stairs—into the church. How about that—everybody stood up, and the organ was playing, and there was no laughing, just crying and staring, and a few of the old and young sisters sobbing, "No, no."

They prayed good prayers about me. Like I was dead but was really alive. That was a switch. Up till now everybody told me I was alive, but I was really dead. Now I'm D.E.A.D., but they tell me I'm alive. Crazy, man, real crazy.

Then the Father got up high over me, laying there in the front of the church, and he said some good things about me. I'm glad somebody had something to say about what was buried down deep inside of me. How I loved my mother and brothers and sisters. O, I loved them. And I didn't hate anybody, man. But, why did they hate me? Man, I felt like I was nobody, going nowhere, and that everybody hated me. I wanted to stand where the Father was standing. I wanted to tell everybody there I loved them. That I wanted to live and be somebody. I didn't want to die. I wanted to live, to be a man like my father was a man. I just wanted to be a man. Why had I been in this box all these years? I felt like I always felt. Nothing new. The box, the top on tight. I couldn't get out, man.

The rats and the roaches, the cold and the stink, the cops and Mr. Charlie, the schools and Uncle Tom, the crooks and the mayor, the landlord and all those good people in church wouldn't let me out. This is no place to be. It's too crowded. I wanted to tell them to be free; to be alive; to hold their heads up high. To get the Man off their back any way that they had to. If he don't get off this box then put him in a box too.

Jesus I'm tired. I wish this was over. The reporters are here; they took pictures of the box and my mother. What more do they want.

It's over now—we're going. Down the aisle, the cross up there in front was carried by one of the guys. Back into the hearse now —the ride along the highway to the grave. Now I'm earth to earth and ashes to ashes. The dirt is under me, around me, and on top of me. Buried, man, not on the hill of the cemetery but down here at the bottom. I'm near the highway. Near the trucks, buses, cars, smells, noises; screaming motors, horns and tires. I'm down here and they're all going now, back to the box with the lid fastened down.

Will any of them come to this place again? I don't know, it really doesn't matter, I guess. I wonder if they will put my name on the top of my grave. They say that every one of us is known by name. Somewhere, maybe.

You know, man, when they carried me out of the church for this last ride, some old white lady on the corner, looking at all the cops and all the people, said, you know what she said, she said, "Somebody very important must have died."

Prayers in Time of War . . .

A LITANY

O God, the peace that passes understanding,
    Help us to understand.
O God, all men living together in love and peace,
    Help us to love peace.
O God, who is hung up in this terrible war in Vietnam,
    Help us to get out.
O God, who is a civilian blown to bits by the bombs which
someone said were only meant to destroy military targets,
    Help us to stop the war.
O God, who wanders alone, lost, crying, scared, no speech from
mouth after your mother and father were ripped to death before
your eyes,
    Help us to stop the war.
O God, who is sold for a lousy buck as a sweet whore in Saigon,
and dies every night and hates her murderers,
    Help us to stop the war.
O God, who staggers from village to village, hut to hut, cave to
cave, unable to outrace destruction,
    Help us to stop the war.

O God, whose town, village, family, friends, children, land, crops, home, are no more,

> Help us to stop the war.

O God, who has a phony election determined by the sword and not the vote,

> Help us to stop the war.

O God, who is a flunkie, taking in some wash, polishing some boots, stealing some supplies, kissing someone's ass to survive, and is dead inside,

> Help us to stop the war.

O God, who has troops and tanks and planes in your land to protect you from yourself,

> Help us to stop the war.

O God, who has the self-appointed Policeman of the world ravaging you and your land,

> Help us to change the Nation.

O God, who is used as the reason for escalating a Third World War, the whim of the militants and fascists of our day,

> Help us to change the Nation.

O God, who is enticed with a chocolate bar in the hand and a knife in the back,

> Help us to stop the war.

O God, who has seen his cities become vile, filthy, corrupt, run for the advantage of your supposed liberators,

> Help us to stop the war.

O God, who is blasphemed by this holocaust of killing,

> Help us to stop the killing.

O God, who is a number every day in the local paper or on the TV screen, 19 of us, 127 of them,

> Help us to stop the killing.

O God, who is us and them?

82

Help us to be.

O God, who is poor and couldn't find a job in the Great Society and got shipped to Vietnam to kill the poor,

Help us to change our sick society.

O God, who is black, put on the front line to kill people of color because we don't discriminate when it comes to killing,

Help us to change our sick society.

O God, who is called "nigger" in the land of the free and the brave, and a freedom fighter in Vietnam,

Help us to change our sick society.

O God, whose black body is twisted still in death in some rice paddy, for free elections in Vietnam, and swinging softly from some tree in the United States because he went to vote in a free election,

Help us to change our sick society.

O God, who is sold a phony bill of goods that he is fighting for democracy and freedom,

Help us to change our sick society.

O God, whose country fights war in the name of self-determination and allows none to the poor of its own land,

Help us to change our sick society.

O God, who has been duped into the paranoia of killing human beings who are called communist instead,

Help us to change our sick society.

O God, who has sold out peace and love and humanity in the name of pride, nationalism, flag waving, support the boys, boys, drop the bomb, kill the Gooks,

Help us to change.

O God, who is hung up knowing the war is wrong but we're there and can't see anyway out and the war grows and grows,

Help us to change.

83

O God, who hates the war, its sickness, its immorality, the unjustness, the calamity, and folly, and is afraid to speak out and act out peace,

> Help us to change you.

O God, who died on the hill, came home in the box, and is now ashes to ashes for what?

> Help us to see you.

O God, who receives a telegram, a visit in uniform, and the words, "We are sorry, your son . . ."

> Help us to know you.

O God, fighting to survive, kill or be killed, and know its all sick and wrong,

> Help us to know you.

O God, who believes we want negotiations and self-determination, when in reality we want surrender and our own way,

> Help us not to be phony.

O God, whose country has made a mockery, and destroyed the United Nations of the world,

> Help us to change the Nation.

O God, whose government has the whole world in fear and terror of impending disaster,

> Help us to change the Nation.

O God, whose government labels those who seek peace, who dissent from their policy as simplistic traitor, giving aid and comfort to the enemy,

> Help us to change the people.

O God, who hears the thunder of war in Vietnam and the silence for freedom in South Africa and Rhodesia,

> Help us to seek freedom.

O God, whose churches too often close their eyes, bless the war, pray for victory in Jesus' name,

Help us to change the Church.

O God, who is told the war is holy, righteous, some kind of divine mission to set the people free,

Help us out of the con game.

PEACE

Where has the peace gone to, Lord?
Where has it gone?
Is it gone forever, Lord?
Did it ever come?
People dying, Lord.
O Lord, they're dying.
The bombs falling, the children crying . . .
      they can't find their mother and their father's dead.
Dead, Lord—plowed down.
Down into the ground and his children are crying. Crying peace.
Let there be peace!
Let the children sing peace, Lord.
Let the people sing peace, Lord.
Let the soldiers sing peace, Lord.
We're ready for dying, Lord, if there's no other way.
But, Lord, I wouldn't kill a man in a war.
I'd just die believing, Lord—and struggling and loving.
Die with my children and my woman, Lord; that's how I'd die.
But I fear dying like that, Lord,

because people would say it didn't make sense.
No sense, they would say, Lord.
They'd say I was no man, dying like that with my children and
my woman, Lord.
That's what they would say.

Would you know, Lord?
I know you would know. Peace!
Amen.

A PRAYER
ABOUT VINCENT McGEE

Somebody stuck a piece of mimeographed paper into my hand.
It talked about justice in America and love of people and putting
away the weapons of killing and using our abundance for all
mankind and not for our own self-interest.
Some guy had put this piece of paper in my hand
     and the guy who said these things on this piece of paper
     was going to prison for not going into the Army and
learning how to kill people.

Some people
     kind of took this piece of paper that was being passed out
     and crushed it in their hand and threw it on the ground—
     like that was the end of it all.
Was that the way it was that Friday up on that hill, Lord?

The guy's name was Vincent McGee, Jr., Lord—
     but then you already know that.
Amen.

THE BANQUET

I know you don't edit *The New York Times,* Lord.
You probably don't even read it.
Some people think the *Times* is the Bible.
You didn't write the Bible either, Lord.
I guess you read it through just to see how they told the story.
Well, the *Times* had an ad in the paper today with a nice
fat-faced child saying she was going to have jumbo shrimp,
Alaska king crab, chicken cacciatore, and a whole lot of other
food in some restaurant.
On the next page
    there was this picture of little skinny-faced and
swollen-bellied kids in Biafra.
They say maybe six million will die soon.
Lord, you know what they can do with their king crab.
I'm sorry, Lord,
    but you just get so sick—
    so little you can do—
    so powerless to change all this misery.

I hope the rich choke on their lobster thermidor—
then they can be with you and those poor kids in heaven.
Amen.

THE NUMBERS GAME

We've got a new number's game going, Lord, in the land of the
free and the brave.
I just turned the radio on, Lord, and got the latest count.
You know, the 11 o'clock news . . .
We get news every hour on the hour,
    or the half-hour,
    or five minutes before the hour,
    or twenty-four hours a day on one station.
That means you can get the count any time you want.

The count tonight was 125 of them and 17 of us.
Like died, Lord.
Just dead.
Now I don't know who they and us are, Lord,
    but I guess they mean 125 poor yellow people who got
killed fighting for their land and their families and their freedom
in Vietnam.
And the 17 is us over here in America
    who got into this war and can't get out.

91

I don't like this "them" and "us" business.
I die every time someone else gets killed.
It's all us dying like people, Lord—
    your children dying.
We should stop the killing of us all, Lord.
"If you did it to the least of these, you did it to me."
We should stop killing you, Lord.
Amen.

NON-VIOLENT,
THEY SAY, LORD

Non-violent, they say, Lord.
That is what we all ought to be, Lord—non-violent.
The President said we should solve our problems with
non-violence.
Why does he order the killing of the poor yellow people in
Vietnam?
Why, Lord?
The President trains troops at home
      to kill the people in the streets when they rebel against
oppression.
He gives medals to men who kill people who are fighting for their
own, Lord, and then calls the blacks of America who fight for
their own liberation,
      criminals.
He says we are fighting for the freedom of the people in Vietnam.
If the President is right, Lord,
      and so many people think he is,
      why doesn't he order an invasion by our troops into Jersey

City, Newark, Birmingham, Selma, South Africa, Rhodesia?
Why not, Lord?
Let's all be free.
Amen.

LOVE, LORD

You know, Lord,
    I hate to see you bleeding and crying and mutilated all over.
You know what I mean:
    all that stuff about all of us being created in your image.
I just don't figure how somebody in your image can kill somebody
else like you, and like them.
It's all crazy, Lord,
    real crazy.
I saw you on television, Lord,
    just standing there and screaming and crying
    and you were just a little boy—maybe seven years old.
Your mother,
    she was just laying in the ditch, dead.
And your father,
    nobody knows where he is.
Maybe in heaven, Lord.
Are all the people who died in Vietnam in heaven, Lord?
I don't know.
Lord, they call it war—

They got a lot of strange names that they use when they talk
about it:

    like bombs; bazooka; F-87s; choppers; napalm; tanks;
gun ships; generals and privates.

The other words are like:

    destruction; starvation; corruption; escalation;
search-and-destroy; killing—like dead, Lord.

Like dead in the name of what, Lord?

They tell me in the name of freedom, Lord.

Now nobody's kidding me

    and I know sure as hell they ain't kidding you.

War is sick, Lord;

    and this war is real sick.

Did you hear, Lord?

We're destroying the people and the things of the people we say
we're helping—

    and we got the world all jumpy and not knowing what we
will do next.

This land of the free and brave which is so short of freedom is
kind of telling everybody else how to be free.

You know, Lord, other people don't like that.

I think a lot of sickness comes from pride and what we call
prestige.

I ain't interested in prestige, Lord.

I'm interested in peace, and freedom, and truth, and justice, and
like human dignity;

    you know—let people decide for themselves.

Something must be wrong somewhere, Lord.

We got men with guns everywhere;

    in Vietnam, in Germany, in France, in Formosa, in Watts,
in Washington.

96

Are all those guns there to make freedom
or keep us from having freedom?
I don't know, Lord.
Do you?
I know you know,
and I guess we all know,
you don't make no freedom with guns.
So Lord,
I got to say to you that this prayer is about getting some real
peace in the world.
It's about ending the war in Vietnam.
It's about letting people make their own decisions.
It's about how sick I feel about all those poor people and
children who are burning up in rice paddies over there or dying
in slums over here.
It's about love.
It's about you, because you are love.
It's about love between brothers and sisters all over this world.
So Lord,
let the screaming of the bombs be still this night—
the soldiers of both sides rise up and know one another as
brothers—
the fire's out—
the guns to speak no more.
The children in your ever-loving arms.
Our country free at last
and the people of the world free at last,
each the way they would have it.
No more killing, Lord.
That would be good, wouldn't it?
Love, Lord!
Amen.

TAPS

They called him Meade, Lord—Frank, Jr.
They named him that when they poured water on his head, and
they said he was signed with the sign of the cross.
He carried it for twenty-two years in the hills of Vermont—
    in the woods,
    in the schools that took him to the fourth grade.
His mother died
    and Frank Sr. lived in a one-room shack
    that was too hot in the summer
    and too hot in the winter.
It was always hot—
    walking 10 miles every day into the woods to cut pulp, and
then walk out.
But the air was clean and the water ran with fish, and Frank Jr.
was his boy.
He went to the fourth grade
    —but you already know that, Lord—
    and they were poor—white-trash poor.
And his country said:

"Poor Frank, Jr., we want you to come with us to Vietnam
and help make a good life for the people. So they can be educated
and free.
Never mind your being white trash—
    you're drafted."

They poured water over him again to clean him off
    and sent his body home to those green hills,
Three weeks in Vietnam,
    then home to the shack where Frank Sr. wipes his eyes and
it makes no sense to him at all.
Poor white trash going into that rich ground of those rich green
mountains.
The poor—
    they die for the rich and go to the rich earth to make it
richer.
They called him Meade, Lord.
Now they call him dead.
You hear, Lord?
Your people are beginning to hear, Lord.
Amen.

O GOD, WHO IS PEACE

O God, who seeks peace and refuses to be called into the army
to learn how to search and destroy and raise the kill ratio,
 Help us to love peace.
O God, who is joining together with others to find ways to end
the war and love peace,
 Help us to organize.
O God, who has marched the streets to bring the troops home, to
stop the bombing, to negotiate, to give Vietnam back to the
Vietnamese, to stop the killing, to stop the war,
 Help us to love peace.
O God, who is organizing to bring some sanity, some love, some
understanding among the people of the nations and the world,
 Help us to love peace.
O God, who would run the risks of peace and not the risks of
war,
 Help us to stop the war.
O God, who loves his country and is horrified to see what it is,
and protests in the hope of changing the nation and its people,
 Help us to stop the war.

100

O God, who has seen the urgency of the day and will risk all for peace,
>Help us to stop the war.

O God, who burns his draft card and loves freedom,
>Help us to love freedom.

O God, who is a pacifist and conscientious objector, and loves peace,
>Help us to love peace.

O God, who burns the flag and loves people,
>Help us to love people.

O God, who refuses to kill his brother in war and sits and rots in prison,
>Help us to stay strong.

O God, who talks to his neighbor, people at work and on the street, to encourage love and peace between nations of the world,
>Help us to spread the word.

O God, all men, women and children who in their own beautiful way work for peace,
>Help us to stop the wars.

O God, all men, women and children who would like to work for peace and are afraid,
>Help us to join the peacemakers.

O God, the peacemaker,
Blessed are the peacemakers.

O God, I see you,
O God, you're crying,
O God, you're wounded,
O God, you're bleeding,
O God, you're dying,

O God, you're dead.
Long live God!
Long live God!

Prayers over the Church . . .

A LITANY

O People, who are two or three gathered together,
    Wake up!
O People, who are two or three gathered together and call
yourself a church,
    Wake up!
O People, who go to church every Sunday and call yourselves
Christians,
    Wake up!
O People, who are holy, clean, respectable, the "good" people
of the community,
    Hear the people cry out.
O People, who love their suburban rich church, its soft rugs, its
soft pews, its soft words,
    Hear the people cry out.
O People, who spend a quarter of a million dollars for some
education buildings, a chapel, a new church,
    Hear the people cry out.
O People, who love one another because you are the same—
white—well-off, righteous, buying guns, praying nice prayers
about nothing,

Love all the people.

O People, gathering the old canned goods from your stuffed pantry shelves and dragging out your old tattered clothes to send to the poor,

Give your life.

O People, gathered together to study about the Indians, the Poor, the Blacks, the Latin Americans, the Africans, in your little classes, with your little books, for your little minds,

Open up your life.

O People, who make a visit to see the poor in the city, the migrant on the farm, and feel just terrible about how bad things are, and go back to your safety and comfort,

Become Poor.

O People, well-fed, well-churched, who support the status quo of our violent nation, our violent police, our violent war, our violence of poor housing, false education, no jobs, no dignity, and condemn the black and white revolutionaries who fight for liberty and justice for all,

Join the fight.

O People, who have made the church a club house of everything superficial, empty, private and closed,

Don't be afraid!

O People, who every Sunday remind themselves that they are created in the image of love,

Take another look.

O People, who pay the suburban preacher a fat share, and don't give a damn what his brother earns in the bowels of the city,

Share the bread.

O People, who invest your money in racist stocks and banks,

See the poor.

O People, who have a study committee for everything that is painful and do nothing but study,
> Share the pain.

O People, who create programs for the poor, without even asking the poor,
> Listen.

O People, who really believe that the poor will be always with us and keep people poor,
> Watch out.

O People, who have rules and regulations to keep the Spirit behind those big stone walls,
> Take down the walls.

O People, who as the suffering of mankind increases, create a new program with a new program for business as usual,
> Suffer.

O People, who keep their power for themselves and never share,
> Share the power.

O People, who talk about suffering, talk about a Cross, and never feel any pain,
> Suffer.

O People, who have made holy men and put them in high places to bless the war, the corrupt city, the brutal police, the unjust system,
> Love the people.

O People, who run summer programs for the poor children and pat their heads and send them home at the end of the day to the hopelessness of it all,
> Love the children.

O People, who disperse your charity from the church food shelves and clothing store and who relieve the guilt of the suburban brothers and sisters,

Love the brothers and sisters.
O People, who call the housing authority, the city hall, the welfare board, for some small favor for the poor, and who love to paternalize the brothers and sisters,

Cut it out.
O People, who are good, sincere and white, running the affairs of black peoples,

Get out of the way.
O People, who work hard in a city church, make a reputation as a fighter for the poor, then get a nice fat job and leave,

Come back.
O People, who count the attendance, count the money, see the people as things—profit and loss,

Love the people.

A PICTURE OF JESUS

Did you look like that, Lord?
What I mean to say is this:
    I saw a picture of you the other day.
You looked so clean.
Your clothes were so white—so very white.
Your face was so white, too.
All clean and antiseptic.
You looked like you were just Martinized, Lord.
You know—pressed and clean.
And your hair looked like you just had a permanent wave,
    and there you were like a big success.

Did you look like that, Lord?
I always had the feeling you lived out with the people in the
streets and roads.
I don't imagine you could keep your clothes or yourself very
clean.
Your skin must have been naturally dark, and burned even more
by the sun.

Maybe you had a strong, hooked nose and were going a little bald.
Did you look like that, Lord?
I don't know
> and it just dooesn't make much difference;
> but you sure weren't a white Anglo-Saxon Protestant.

My prayer to you, Lord,
> is to thank you for being so beautiful a person in what you said and how you lived.

That's a real picture of you
> and the one we all need to see. Help us to see you *real*, Lord.

Amen.

THE CHIEF APOSTLES

Some guys seem to have it made Lord.
I mean, your chief apostles got it made, Lord.
They live in nice big houses, with nice furniture and good food,
Lord.
Fasting is when you're poor
      and your apostles ain't poor, Lord.
Only the poor fast now, Lord.
They call it malnutrition and starvation.
They don't call your apostles "apostles" much anymore.
They're priests, ministers and rabbis.
They say you were all three, but I think that's to cover their thing.
Then, Lord, they got cars—some guys have real big cars and
they dress like they never got dirty in their life.
People pay most of their bills, Lord—gas, light, insurance,
telephone.
They call them servants.
Can you beat that, Lord?
A lot of the people they priest and minister and rabbi to don't
have that kind of thing.

111

It's nice being taken care of by Mother Church, Lord.
Maybe you don't get rich Lord, but some do, and then in some of
the churches they pay different.
If you're like a bishop you may make $20,000.
Some preachers make $50,000 or more—
     some make $3,000.
Those Christian brothers know how to share the bread, Lord.
And a lot of money Mother Church makes to keep her
professional people safe she makes by owning lots of property
and investing in big business and industry and some racist stuff
too.
If your Church would sell all that it has and follow you, that
would be something.
When do you think they're going to do that, Lord?
Amen.

112

DID YOU HEAR ABOUT IT, LORD?

Did you hear about it, Lord?
Your church had one of those big meetings about us again.
You know, about the poor.
They don't think we can do anything for ourselves
    so they had a lot of real smart people to run the meeting.
People who aren't poor.
They're always doing that, Lord.
They never listen to the poor or give them a chance to speak.
Your church is so rich now, Lord,
    they hardly even know who the poor are.
Lord, I was thinking the other day
    maybe that's why the church pays so little attention to what
you said—
    you were poor.
Amen.

I JUST WALKED OUT, LORD

I just got up and walked out, Lord.
Well, it wasn't exactly like that, Lord.
I said a few things first.
You know how people are when they are feeling things real
strong and real deep and have to run it off at the mouth.
Well, I got up in front of all those delegates at the Church
Convention
    and said it and walked out.
You know, Lord,
    the Convention said Civil Rights is a fad.
How do you like that?
And you living and dying for justice!
They also took a peace resolution and laid it on the table.
This Church of yours laid peace on the table.
This Church of yours laid peace on the table and you put it up
on a cross.
Now if that wasn't bad enough,
    they don't want 700,000,000 Chinese in the United Nations,
so they laid seven hundred million people on the table.

114

How the hell do you lay seven hundred million people on a
table?
It was just sick, Lord,
     and that's what I told them,
     and I said the Church isn't dying—it's dead.
And then I walked out.
It was a long lonely walk down that aisle
     and then I was outside all alone.
I sat down and I knew you were there with me.
I also knew you were still inside that Church at that convention.
Thank you for giving me the guts to say what I said and to walk
out and for coming with me.
And thanks for staying inside with everyone—
     we all need you so bad.
I love you for that.
Amen.

SHAKE UP THE GOOD PEOPLE

Lord, you can hear us praying now,
    right now,
    for all the good people.
You know there are too many good people.
There are a lot more good people than there are bad people.
I think that's our problem, Lord.
Not that there aren't more bad people but that there are so many
good people.
Our city has a lot of good people.
They never bother anyone,
    least of all themselves, Lord.
They never bother themselves about anyone or anything.
Now right there is the source of a lot of problems.
Now, Lord, I hope you will send a lot of people into the city to
bother the hell out of the good people.
You know, shake them up;
    get them to start bothering about other people.
You know, Lord,
    parts of this city

just aren't fit for you to live in.
And some of your good people
should do something about *that,*
shouldn't they, Lord?
Amen.

FOR BISHOPS

God knows bishops need our prayers.
Real prayers.
It must be hard to be so important:
   to be a bishop—one of your most chosen ones, Lord.
So much responsibility, power, position;
   concern is a real burden, Lord.
Now, Lord,
   when men get so much responsibility and position, they
sometimes get scared.
A bishop shouldn't be scared, Lord.
He should be powerful and fearless in love and truth.
So, Lord,
   help all bishops not to be mealy-mouths,
   or too timid and afraid to live and die for truth, freedom and
love.
How come,
   when so many people are sitting in jail and suffering for love
and justice for all men,
so many bishops are sitting in cathedral offices?
Lord,

get all your bishops out in the streets where the people are—
    your people, Lord.
Help them to walk among us and be one with us.
I think they would like to.
Lord, help them not to be afraid.
Help them to know we love them
    and we need them and want them.
Now!
Amen.

ONE FLOCK

Dear Jesus,

    there are a whole lot of people around this neighborhood
here in the city who are christians.

They all say you are the Shepherd of the flock.

And they all say there is one flock.

Now, Lord,

    what's so hard to figure out is why there are so many folds.
There are the Romans, the Episcopalians—as a matter of fact,
more than one Episcopal fold in the neighborhood; the
Presbyterians; the Lutherans; the Baptists; the Methodists—a
couple of them, too; and a whole lot of store-front churches.

Now, Lord, there always has to be room not to be always the
same.

And then christians love their churches very much—

    especially the stained-glass windows,

    or the music,

    or the altar.

Now, Lord,

    what this prayer is all about

is to ask you to help us to be one flock in one fold with you
as the Shepherd.
Then maybe we will all love you and one another,
    and not a building or a denomination.
One church, the Shepherd and his sheep.
That would be very good, Lord,
    because so many sheep can't see the shepherd any more.
There are so many folds in the way.
Amen.

ALL THOSE STUDENTS, LORD

All those students messing up all those hallowed halls, Lord!
Running around talking about ending the war,
    having sit-ins for racial equality,
    saying that diplomas don't make you human,
    that success isn't being on the board of Chase Manhattan;
    saying we should share our wealth with all the people—
    crazy, Lord, just crazy.
The christians aren't for those things, Lord.
The students are embarrassing the Church and the christians,
Lord,
    by all their honesty and guts,
    because the christians just aren't going to deny themselves
anything and take up any cross.
That's just talk.
The people are moving, Lord, and making the christians look
bad.
Keep up the good work, Lord.
Amen.

O PEOPLE

O People, who are sick of their church and its fine comfortable
self-righteous people and have left,
  Join the people.
O People, who see the failure of their churches and so struggle
and try to change them to bring them into the real world,
  Change the church.
O People, who create a new church in their hearts, minds, souls,
and actions in the affairs of men,
  Build the new church.
O People, from every branch of the church who gather together
everywhere in the name of all the brothers and sisters,
  Be Brothers and Sisters.
O People, who voluntarily surrender and share their power with
the people,
  Love the people.
O People, who get out of the way so that other people can do
their thing in beauty and truth,
  Do your thing in beauty and truth.
O People, in the church who are open to those outside,

Open all your doors.
O People, who become poor like Jesus did and share their destiny
with the sufferers of the world,
   Suffer with the people.
O People, who live and act for justice, who see the evil of
oppression and arm themselves in the spirit of their destiny,
   Hold up your arms.
O People, joined together in love, in some basement, some
house, some field, to sing, pray and share the bread of their
humanity,
   The Bread is beautiful.
O People, you're hungry,
   We gave a couple of cans of food.
O People, you're thirsty,
   We gave you two bits for cheap wine.
O People, you're in prison,
   We gave you a record for the rest of your life.
O People, you're naked,
   We gave you second-hand clothes.
O People, you are strangers to us,
   We kept you outside.
O People, poor, hungry, thirsty, in prison, naked, a stranger,
   Help!
O People, poor, hungry, thirsty, imprisoned, naked, a stranger,
   Help!
O People, we were just trying to live, to be alive, to be a man,
   Be the People.
O God the People.
We shall be the people.
Amen.

124

A LOT OF PEOPLE DIG YOU, LORD

A whole lot of people dig you, Lord.
A lot more people than it looks like.
The reason that it's so hard to see so many of the people who love
you and follow you is that they're not in the church.
They believe you were for real
    and they're trying to be like you.
I thought you would like to know that
    in case you don't already know.
It ain't all lost, Lord.
There's still the Kingdom in front of us and all around us.
You overcame it all
    even though you got hung up on that wood.
Help us to overcome our hang-ups too.
Amen.

THE LIVING WORD

Everybody is writing books these days, Lord.
Instead of doing something,
    write a book.
They even published these prayers, Lord.

If all the money, time and energy spent on books could be put
together to make a revolution—
    I mean a real revolution, Lord, for justice—
    that would be a living book.
A lot of your followers think you're a book, Lord.
They quote the book all the time
    and tell me if I don't believe the book, I don't know you.
There are a lot of people hung up on books
    when they should be up tight with people, Lord.
You didn't write any books.
You were a Living Word.
Help us to live, Lord.
Amen.